MILES PRESS

Indiana University South Bend Department of English

GROSS
ARDOR

42 Miles Press
Editor, David Dodd Lee
Copyright© 2013 Bill Rasmovicz. All rights reserved.
ISBN 978-0-9830747-3-1 (pbk. alk. paper)

For permission, required to reprint or broadcast more than several lines, write to:
42 Miles Press, Department of English, Indiana University South Bend
1700 Mishawaka Avenue, South Bend, IN 46615

http://42miles.wordpress.com

Art Direction: Christopher Fox, Design: Fehren Johnson, Production: Paul Sizer
The Design Center, Frostic School Of Art, Western Michigan University.
Printing: McNaughton & Gunn, Inc.

GROSS ARDOR

POEMS
BY
BILL
RASMOVICZ

CONTENTS

I hear the human linen being torn like a great leaf—

—Andre Breton

BENEATH THE FACE IS A BALL PEEN HAMMER

Beneath the face is a ball peen hammer.
Beneath that, core of iron ore.

A face is a guise not unlike an empty barge.
A barge, not unlike a block of lead.

It is thought the fist can squeeze itself
into a bloody pulp, that the body itself is a
Guernica, the sphincter of the lips

a tourniquet for screaming where the tongue
is borne by an annihilation of graces.
If anything it's a centrifuge we're in,
the starling's skin mostly blacktop.

There are degrees of overcast in which
you could drown. Should.
Also, ancestral lines whose bones wither to
the consistency of milk.

Light can be the barber's razor stroking your
cheek, a foreign country
of gyroscopic spires and flaming azaleas,

and sometimes it is not enough
to feel the wind's holy tenor in an empty
lot. No, even the sun heaving up

through its shock of silence sounds
as though someone were pushed
through a window. This is that window.

THE MOON'S HIND LEGS

The moon's hind legs are invisible.
Its bastard ear-boring cry is only fully heard by infants.

Bright as the starchy pharmacist's coat, its objective
is to illuminate the puddled glass replacing
someone's stolen vehicle,

the tuft of fur in the barbed wire.
Some nights it shivers as though it held
a penny under its tongue.

If the eyes were windows at all they would
be fogged 300 days a year.

I understand and I don't:
the past is such an indelible part of now,
that there is no such thing as the edge's gleam
without the cut,

that if nothing else, we endure ourselves.

You love in excess or pine to be loved,
glisten in the rain like a freshly cut stump.
When I saw the tattoo of a hummingbird on

that girl's lonely wrist, I was convinced the skeleton
of that animal would be the topographical account
of an ancient city.
That I would want to live there someday,
bereft, yes, but somehow filled.

To walk beneath it is to ascertain the world's
slow attrition, to know
there is always a self further buried in the self.

Figure ice raking a river bank.
Figure a semi jackknifed on the highway, its cargo
of guinea hens leaking—scripture of the moon.

And this I remember:
wheeling food to the cancer ward's incandescent hall,
patients wading through
its powdery, almost sublime surface;

the scientific odor smuggled via elevator
into the lobby.

That the idea of something so pure is synonymous
with its breaking.

That you could set fire to yourself and the chill
would never leave.

What any of us would suffer for a little affection
or money.

In its countenance the cemetery trees stand
so still, and still they seem to sway.

This morning, the students climbing onto the bus,
one after the next, their faces rained-out
beach vacations,
the garbage bags a street-side abacus

where a man was found after two nights
in the delirium of shallow woods behind his house,
unknown to himself
and white as the rescuer's light.

LIGHT THROUGH A STAR-SHAPED WINDOW

The body not equal to the sum of
its parts, it is natural to love something more
than it can be loved.
When they put you down in the ground, do you believe
you'll grow back as moss on a rock, tree bark?

With the baby gone blue in his crib, no one
knew what to do. So the skull is a rectory of baboons trashing
the furniture and stealing the booze.
For a month the bee lay on its back in the shop's
fluorescent window, its legs antennae
for a distant, unknown signal.

A cockroach under the bed, flood-lines on our foreheads:
living, they say.
If you stare into the pharaoh's eye
of a streetlight, it reveals behind its cankered sheath

that to exude your own Christ-like light would only
summon moths, or the police.
Whether inflection or innuendo, now the hills are farms,
now the farms are terraced porticos
under which the *foie gras* is set to spoil:

not heaven, but a seaside resort for heathens.
Not starlight, but light through a star-shaped window.
Just resting the sheets over your toes can hurt.

It was from the tram window that I saw the man
lope around back, emptying himself behind the museum's
bushes. Meaning the ancient forest lies
somewhere deep within, and anger
is nourishment like absence is an entity that fills us.

GROWTH NOT THE EQUIVALENT OF LONGEVITY

A train pushing underground as the syringe pushes
morphine. Clouds wolfly tread by.

If there is a color to the mind it is wheat brown.
Have you ever felt the shadow of a plane
fly over you, a bell simmering in the afternoon's *au jus*?
At which point it seems perfectly imaginable

you could step out of yourself and walk,
leave the molted skin of a life crumpled behind.

Thinking back, I used to hear gunshots every night—
I'd lie on my bed counting the seconds between pulses
of rapid-fire, waiting for the paramedics.

Some people exist in a mild strobe, radiant yet calm.
Others are happier in heartache and penance. And some
find it inconceivable to live anywhere but
within spitting distance of the volcano.

Once, a guy died on my doorstep, though I was away
for the weekend. Anxiety it turns out
is a family of badgers
clawing at the den of your ribs.

When studied long enough, all things acquire human
form. I think of silence now as a kind of
negative space, an almost neonatal scream.

It's suggested that to find your place in the world,
there is already a dialogue, you just have to build on it.
While some thoughts turn into gestures alone:

the long green swoon of a tulip, head bowed
for the four-year-old fingers of the executioner.

THE STUDY OF LYMPH

One life is always the culmination of many.
We are a serious people,
on hands and knees we have rubbed the cat hair
from the rugs. The brightness (meaning star)

by which we navigate is a large hospital. It is the psyche
that is such fissile material,

the chemical scent of cleanliness our agent of calm.
Someone must make a career of their hair. Inevitably,

someone thick with goiter must leaf-sweep the pool.
Who will construct the bridges & highways out of here?
Who will care for us upon expiring?

A life in the forest must be considered, pops the wren
branch to sun-spackled branch,
so too the baby's wailing through the wall regarded
as modern opera. Somehow the limbs

always know where the other limbs are, yet
the organ housing the emotions is a border city between
nowhere and nowhere.
And where belief is most pronounced there is war,

and war against it. Buddha's path
was to let the meatwheel turn.
As the way of money is to let the meatwheel turn.

Against nature
is to do what's in your own best interest.
Like burning the villagers' homes with them inside was
a way to say *Leave!*
and yet they couldn't just say it.

TRUTH IS A GORILLA SUIT

Truth is what it feels like to wreck on a road of red
packed ash at fifty miles an hour. Forgive us

our ears the *a priori* hiss of ether dissipating.
Think of a glue extracted from your bones, a hacksaw
resonating in your fillings. This evening

is a sentiment you can walk through
laced with strychnine and foaming at the shore,

a window, the mathematical symbol dividing *out there* by
in here. You can say a whole lot
with a single match,

like throwing bullets into a fire is a kind of gun.
You can get away with so much more

if you can run. If the heart beats at all it beats outwardly.
At the center of which is what?

Does it produce a wave radiating to other people in the room?
Or dissolve back into the body, neither
created nor destroyed?

Shadows of crows ricochet off the walls in the house.
A millionth of a degree and half a moment later,

a chemical change has taken place.
Bull horns in the middle of the night collapse onto your plastic
piano. A helicopter hovers over you

as you sleep. You hammer your thumb, succumb
to a scorpion in your shoe.

Yes, we are on a huge coal-cracking conveyor belt.
Yes, we are on horseback, backwards and blindfolded
toward an undisclosed location.

First they haul you out and sever the cord. Then
they immediately swaddle you in white to stain the blood.

THE VISCSOSITY OF MARROW

She says sleeping next to the boiler room is no solace
with its pressure like a hive of
simmering hornets. After which, she reasons

the only species that will survive us
are rats, cockroaches, scorpions and possibly bologna.

She demands to know exactly what process it is
we've engaged; fission or fusion, putrefaction or symbiosis.

Her life, she shrinkingly offers, has the experiential novelty
of a seahorse's. Her desire?
To be as valid as jackhammer dust.

I tell her sometimes I wish I could don a mustache of pure Adriatic
fog, begin again in the mud, simple as a newt.

We argue the mercurochrome sky as radiant
and irradiated. Though we agree that one cannot know

all facets of the body and remain body, that we all adhere
to a kind of watery, subterranean music.

She folds her underwear with the grace required
to hem a mosquito wing.
I leave my stubble in the sink.

She wonders about the viscosity of marrow,
whether the labyrinthine assembly of a French horn
is necessary, if we're merely

a context for each other.
She allows me to sleep next to her, suspecting that

in the middle of the night, if the flint of our lips
ever struck, we would consume each other, or be consumed.

THE LOVELIEST CITIES

A tree hides in the shiver of its leaves
while vines take to its scaffolding to suffocate it.

The dead offer us their sympathy, which is to say
their silence. The dead are a lot like the living
except they don't say much. And what is

the heart but a telephone fluttering with a bomb
threat, love being if you carry the cross of my affection
I'll carry yours.

I recall shouting down into the mine's air shaft
to hear myself. What rose was exponential
in size and someone else entirely.
There were days whose sweet musk was the warm body
of a violin's, the wind

a girl whispering through the parish yards for her cat.
Now it's consecration by hail, the beaming effrontery
of the wrecking ball.

At the core of the mind is an obelisk dreaming you
into being. Jumping off the roof, I still think an open
umbrella would save me. And we wonder:
whose shoes were found behind

the rest stop? Murk, the barrel of a rifle—
to peer where you can't see bottom, witness something
solid as earth liquefy. There is no discerning

a sparrow from sky really, each of which
without the other would fall. While the loveliest cities
have civilizations compounded into geologic strata

topped with screaming police lights and children
separated from their parents.
Which is to say we are phantoms of each other,
that the end is always happening.

FIELDS NEWLY TURNED

I'm a sparrow in a man's body,
pollen on the placid Arno, empty calories

in the mouth of a trout.
Already I'm sick of the Apennines' furloughed
breezes. My breaths are as enormous and
complicated as the emperor's. These newly-turned

fields are the barber's perfect comb-over.
Dear window frame in which
the birds bathe in the dewy grasses, would I be
more handsome with a bone through my nose?
I think I can hear insects nibbling the clover.

To have learned anything at all
is to know the temperature by degrees of
swelling in your knees, O that if everything were
good and right we would be as equally fucked.

Which is otherwise to say that removing the arrows
is to push them all the way through.

Dear pitch black, why are the moths' trajectories
so inaccurate around the source cauterizing
wing with wing? I should take a pill, take a lunch—

it is important you know to have lunch
among the graves, to have lived on nothing

but the buzz of the yellow-jacket hovering
in the rose's white pocket, to know that
rich as the soil is, it needs the pig's blood
for the trees to be green.

And you, does your head swivel like an owl's yet?
Does the body instinctively follow?
Here may be the perennial nosebleed
you've been looking for.

MIGRATIONS WRESTED

Water underground is tireless.
Where snow has melted, geese feed from the softness.

Whose head isn't wobbly as an ox's on a stick-figure spine?
Whose skin isn't a natural quarantine to the natural world?

Cinematically roving, the park was a graveyard without graves
in which we craved the mulched scent of Christmas trees,
an air mezzo formal
like the lawyer had allotted a single afternoon, beyond which
a firm decision was required.

On the hospital's sixth floor, machines labored forth
the sound of digital moss. Still, it was impossible to coax the
hermit crab from its shell with another shell.

The vivisected head of the plastic baby doll lay next to
an ice-ladder pondside.
The moon's umbilicus dangled freely in daylight too bright to see.

How to come to your name as your own?
When the washing machine cracked the bricks holding it up. . .
And doctor of anything was half of what a dandelion root knew. . .

True: the rug's arabesque was no longer emblematic of living.
Aesthetics, too, were scientific laws obeyed & broken.
You created your own weather system by entering a room.

Beneath, the bones of the dead seemed simply
bones of the deep dead, the glee of sledders' sentences
like doors too heavy for hinges.

My words were your words, my growling bowels
your growling bowels.
Either the geese were always there, or they would never leave.

This was our dream, that an afternoon amidst sycamores
and they would take us for their own.

THE SOVEREIGN RICHNESS OF DEFEAT

The dogs want the stick the woman is throwing
and are disenchanted when she throws the stick,

while the robot's blood is thick as a jelly donut.
In this episode, the man at the window
is on an important call, staring at the wing tips' glare.

Beyond the terminal's thick glass and his glasses,
clouds fumble in and out of place, atmospheric puzzle.
His posture suggests he is happy for his suitcase with

wheels, the preponderance of cupcake shops in this city.
The aircraft are mathematically poised to inform us
nothing is random in this world, that

the microbes are steadily at work beneath our
fingernails. Just look at our perfectly machined teeth!

Loss, if we're talking about the emotions, is something
communicable via the ether, from
one far away person to another.
A failed submarine, it could float
to the bottom of your cellular unknown.

There is you. There is I. Then there is us.
The man at the glass is a composite.

The wildebeest locked in the water's grip on screen,
the museums documenting a comfort in hardship
like what the weathered facades of buildings imply
by remaining—

no one knows what to do when the vertigo is over,
what to say, or to whom.

One thinks the air cannot distribute demeanor from
me to you but it can, that there are
only a few lives within us to acquire or give up.

IN THE HEMISPHERE BETWEEN QUEST AND CONQUEST

Dew makes the green swell and pop, humble architect
of the psyche.
The bumblebee debates between horseshit
and lilac, and bronze we come to find

is not a metal or color but a mood.
Surrendered here, the congress of our emotions, the parentheses
of skin too permeable to mosquitoes, infrared.

This morning the goldfinch at the foot of the house
mistook the reflection of birch trees in the wind for
birch trees in the wind. I get to thinking

that these silly appendages are but the spirit's prostheses,
that the tanker anchored in the harbor only espouses

the firmament of meaning
because there is none. Every morning a man ascends the hill
to strike the noontime bell. The church
emotes in the scent of honeysuckle.

That their attributes might continue with us, once they consumed
the dried powder of dead relatives.
Now, candles are passed to every table at dusk,
the jacket without its body there on a hook.

To feel god-like, like a box of nails, a salt lick—
the inhabitants' itinerary remains: carry a flower in the wind,
stare at the sun without going blind.

THE EVIDENCE

The air choked with cottonwood dander
and tranquilizer blue.
From the crevice of a rock wall, a fist of wildflowers
sucker-punching the nothing.
People toting cameras and beers

equaling some inebriated form of truth-equals-beauty.
In the broken cathedral
a windowless window frames the notion that
what's gone is gone, evidence
that evidence of ourselves sometimes suggests otherwise.

In the field behind, a child runs, hair flagging the calm,
her face apple-red and the stinger
still in her heel.
The imprint she leaves in the grass someone
later says must have been a small deer's.

EMERGENCY THEORY

There was no reason to halt the picnic.
A tennis-ball-size tumor swung from the spaniel's
abdomen. Who-doing-whom rumors
quivered the topiaries

and the grill's rusted pin-width axles screeched
for milk, or lubrication.

So the bandage requires the wound to ooze.
So the hospital beds must be occupied, as a profit is
necessary, and the CEO's exotic auto.

So the sausage grease spews into the coals as
an homage to volatility,

like the orange tape wound round orange
cones, elevating in circumstance the street's sinkhole.

To anyone watching,
we were a gladiatorial combat spectacle
as rust was to a slow burn—
clouds couched in a craft, the light
swollen-libido-pink on the posh apartment complex.

The soft waves that canoodled your toes two weeks ago
no longer mattered.

Queer it was that distortion from the humming wires
could make a note more emotionally acute, truer
to the experience,
or equally an experience.

Disdain lingered, like when you passed a dead
fawn on the highway.

Gone was the urge to mouth meat from bone.
Gone was urgency.
No kids, no pets, plastic utensils—

didn't the spirit need resistance against which
to hone itself?

The new suit would not mandate your new career.
Or it might.
It was essential, as conclusions went, to pray your
innards to the television or some new music or
god of friends of friends.

So the spat fingernails and torn cuticles
would persist,
and the human remains upon x-ray in the suspect's
gut turn out to be chickens' feet.

Mayonnaise like sun-block on our lips, we stood there
middle-fingering an annihilation or new world
somehow immanent, baffled at ourselves

and our selves,
as the wincing cardiac lights up the alley
towards someone's busted kidney or
collapsed lung, whatever it was, continued.

LIGHTHOUSE IN PODONK

The child is thrown by her beloved steed
and thusly the world enters. The first act is always
a deathtrap. Brutish ambience meted by a grammar of
flowers as an appeal to the personal.

Elsewhere in the wild, the hardest part of making
the skull a showpiece is stripping the meat
from bone, kind of like saying what you think.
No. Saying what you think is like taxidermy,

stuffing the dead deer and standing it in your living
room, as if the living room were a forest.
I for one attest to the vatic council of leaves as a circuitry

without wires straight to the brain, the strange erasures
when wind blows.
What's empirical when the past is no longer?
Dead-ending river, meet billboard horizon.

Horizon, you're nothing but a heady byproduct of
scorch and asphalt. And all the inhabitants want is
to trust their ashes will be scattered in a bright blue
corner of the sea when they die.

O If I could phosphoresce. . . like the penitentiary light's
tanning bed orange illuminating
if only the panties stolen from the clothesline. . .

The sincerest thing I ever saw was the hunchbacked
woman hauling her loaf of bread. That arc of stairs to
exponential stairs, her plodding ascent,

she was more concrete than concrete. Suddenly
the carapace of the world is lifted.
Friends, if it only means what it feels then those feathers
you have for guts are real, simple

as snow is its own language. Even if, buried beneath an
expanse of blizzard-princess white, heart
is a euphemism for blood diamond.

BUTTERFLY HUNTING

If I could haul drowning Venice ashore by its ear, wear
the spotted pelt of the suburban night.
If I could only remember to put the toilet seat
down, buy flowers.

Have you ever wondered why the brain resembles
a meat umbrella?
Have you ever stared at the sky until a cloud began?

The buildings splinter this way & that, sirens pass
and sap bleeds from the trees,
and the way the tarmac shivers in the distance purports
a world multiplying itself by itself.
What I'm afraid of

are the prospects for human-headed lettuce,
mothballs filling the ice tray.
I suspect the heart is a tiny owl.
I'm suspicious of what the mind acquires *in utero*.
I think I'm becoming a solitary beam of ghetto light.

O *ennui* is only another form of rapture,
the serenity of water, to watch it succumbing to its own
forces. I believe there is a space in which everything
is essential, that the line between shadow
and person is seamless.
I know there is nothing more ornate than
a hard blow to the shins.

The arms, the legs, they could be the recycled scraps of
ladder from the coal cellar.
The bridge buckling beneath us, a thousand years
compressed into the head of a pin, and pictures
to prove it. Come, let us walk.

SECRETS OF BREATHING

The little cloud of depression in the anti-depressant commercial
looks like Wittgenstein's aura,
looks like my brother smoldering up from the grave.

Respite in the park, anyone?
Let's all go for a milkshake then hold hands afterwards,
maybe sit on the swings for a while so our feet can breathe.

One secret is to be exceptional with your hands
or brilliant at diagnosing animals,
limber enough to fit inside the washing machine should
anyone come looking for you.
Remember the movie where they rendered light

into a substance like pudding, like oozing actual thought?
Sometimes you think just by thinking it, it rains harder,
that somehow you are and always were.
People say to have on a nice watch at your time of death,
a wad of cash on hand for the afterlife,

that carrion overhead will cause the cornice of your eyebrow to itch.
What we're after in this life we couldn't even say,
warm sox, untouched forest
with berries whose deliciousness would make your head pop off,
to reconcile human sacrifice as part of our ancient repertoire
alongside a preference for juice without the pulp.

There is no greater silence than that of people listening.
No richer decibel than your neighbor's bedroom being shelled.

Look how the opportunity for us to meld into the future
passes second by second, just by mentioning it.
Did you ever feel your arms were winter-worn branches?
What does it mean to have blood-tinged urine in your dream?

I come home from work and water the TV, maybe turn on the plants,
consider the Santas buoyed to the roofs,
the deer in the enormity of sleep,

and all the facts become obsolete.
The articles of memory fold up like paper birds and are gone.
It's getting creepy in here, I think: *Terra Incommunicado*.

And then I hear, like something turned inside out
in the underbrush, like a cockatiel with its diamond
tipped beak on antiquated vinyl—HAIL, AMERICA, VICTORIOUS!

RESONANT FREQUENCY

The muscles can outlast the tendons, the tendons
bone, bone any memory you can lay claim to.

Weeding the garden is a brutal endeavor, it turns out,
though if by virtue of the food you consume *you are*

then O what candied experience is sure to manifest
after double dosing on chocolate tort afterwards.
A bonfire of the senses, that's what we're after,

a sort of ceremonial wandering through the wilderness,
finally determining whether you're covering hallowed
ground with your years, or are merely ground cover.

It is difficult to understand. Eating the sweetbreads of
their enemy, some tribesmen believed they would

know better. Surely it was over the calf's supple thymus
Antonio Stradivari thought his instruments could

extract and amplify the resonant frequency of the forest,
that layering spruce, willow, and maple, a violin
could subdue an audience as if
by a map of their emotional pressure points.

So many things can make you weep, change your viewpoint
entirely, like the goldfish on the counter in its upside-down
faux space helmet, now banned in some Italian towns
because the glass's arc distorts the fish's view of reality,

rendering the medieval hilltop town a metropolis,
thereby making its inhabitants feel miniscule,
like the notion resurfacing in whatever cardboard box,
biosphere, or personal prefect you inhabit

where you are the tiniest of organelles, know
almost nothing, while allotted the lifespan of a mayfly.

HELSINKI

Helsinki hugs the ground as though the heavy sky
has compressed it.
I wonder, do the heavens too pray that the heavens
don't rain down on them?

One postulation is that the shadow is an apparitional crowbar
to leverage you into the world,
reminder for times of vapid presence.

Photographs show half of one's face consumed—a mouth
without lips, tongue, or teeth
devouring us.

Have you ever been mistaken by a moth for lamplight?
Can you not sense the magnitude of its
shadow-borne wings?

Look into the eye of a horse—horses are nothing but shadow.
And have you ever seen the shadow
of smoke?

Today is like someone's empty briefcase spilled open
into the streets,
the preoccupations of people just walking
where even a life long lived is not necessarily living.

At times I think of myself as a river.
A river is a shadow.

A cloud weighs no more than air and has a shadow,
while a star has none.

A river sounds like Rachmaninoff on the keys of a dead piano,
a kind of loud subterfuge.

Sometimes voice is a river.
Sometimes words are heavier than their actual weight,
like the energy from the mass in a paperclip

can lift a cargo ship clear out of the water.
Even the translucence of a window
makes a shadow; the afternoon cracked and fallen
from its frame.

I am told that emotional weight is the heaviest.
I too believe the suggestion of a thing
is often more convincing than the thing itself,

that a dark shade of gray is by far the most complex
in the spectrum of human emotion.

I am told that with the shovel of its beak
the buzzard will bury itself.
Have you ever seen your face in the holy schism of a tree?

One morning you wake,
and wake again to where a building was,
now an empty lot.

Standing there is the memory of a building,
the woman in tears staring up long after it has burned.

Ø Ø Ø

IN THE FOREST YOUR MOOD IS THE COLOR OF THE TREES

In the scree of an avalanche
it is impossible to know whether you're upside down
or even sideways. Just walking through open air

induces effects of rope burn.
I remember the woman getting knocked from her shoes
stepping into traffic. It was as if she were still standing
right there, but you could see clear through to

the bowling alley's empty parking lot.
If only we could plan such exit strategies.

In a crevasse between tenements,
a hollow furnace as metal drum for the rain.
Or, what you'd hear cupping your ear to the window.

In another life the kneecaps will make perfect ashtrays.

Have you ever stuffed your arm in the carcass of a deer?

And on the table, why was the fruit always left to rot?

Eventually landscape summers the hillside
revolution green, the river ambles away
water-drunk on itself,

and what you trophied as love turns out
was a chance encounter amidst superior produce.

I've seen death's wooden cart stuck in the mud
amidst the black grapes, heard windows crashing
that insinuate the husk of someone fleeing themself.
Anecdote:

for four months there has been a spoon outside
on the windowsill. I have tried
and neither will it evaporate nor combust.

YOU CAN ALMOST SEE THE OCEAN FROM HERE

To differentiate between fire and flame
one must offer the self.

Sebastian, he let the arrows pierce him into ecstasy.
At least that's what Gozzoli revealed—
that perma-grin, that attitude exuded in the astute
pitch of his hip.

Despite our capacity to outshine the godhead himself,
the body is to be spent.
Any imaginable Shangri-La then

is just an incarnation of someone else's Gulag.
So it is, that the ethics of desire need not apply
for chemical welfare,

that, leg gashed, the man perennially seeking change
outside the drugstore smiles wider than you.

What are any of us a bad dream couldn't set straight,
a day in the mines?
From the moment of our outset it was known,

doubt is a stone you swallow, rain
a multiplication by many zeros, and the hip or
spine is always the first to go.

And all you're inspired to do is catch up with your
couch and drown in a video of the ocean
on your ocean-sized television.

Keep believing you are elsewhere.
Keep forgetting air has weight.

An empire will pull itself into existence by
the straps of its own two boots.
The beard can grow so thick
you can no longer force sustenance though it.

FROM GULLS SALVAGING OPEN AIR TO HYPERVENTILATION

Upon visitation, her muscles had atrophied.
A giant pumpkin, she was confined to herself by

herself in the nursing home's high field. Outside, rain
pelting the leaves was a referendum
for everyone to shut up.

Rain: people say stones have more aesthetic value
in the rain,
that the language of futility is rain.

I keep hearing the footsteps of the conquerors.
I keep thinking my head is an estuary of bees.

Trying to decipher your life from your life
you're left with a monkey's paw in your dresser drawer
and the foreign currency of
having exoticized yourself abroad.

Everyone wished to know:
how to get past the gleam of an hour prior like
the museum's fetus in a jar.

If the first telescope was a soap bubble lodged in a femur. . .

If wisdom manifests as profuse hair from your nose and ears. . .

and the most serene sky
is where the eyes turn back inside their head. . .

If the future of humankind is machinery. . .

who could account for the days
were they not concretized in the calendar's prison grid?

We were pawns in a bone shop, gulls in a snow.

What we need is a hunger for vertigo.

Remember the blossoms the wind tore in two,
Regulus on sunny shore, sans eyelids.
Fortunate to have a passion through it all, passion we did.

OBLIQUERY

The deer just stood there, lethargic yet iconic,
a wanderlust of calm.
When they moved, it was in Ouija-like algorithms, each of
their perambulations a function of the other's.

Far away obliterations were going on.
Like pods of leaking milkweed, easy enough, there were
actual people that vanished
only to end up the ink blot on a milk carton,
blood relatives I wouldn't recognize right in front of me.

Whatever it takes to make the dead swoon back into
the arboretum, I thought. Here
was land neither of us wanted to own or be buried in.

In the forest deep
deer shit was sprouting Christmas trees.
With which, we could calculate our speed, hence efficiency
toward neverendingness.
Under the power-lines we agreed not to have babies.

And the retrospect we ascribed to waste therefore was.
How we abandoned the fledgling garden for a vacation in Hvar,
the few apples on the branch whose fruit was
siphoned back to feed the tree,
the tree, form sky had sucked the marrow from.

Or such was our composure, massive and duly
minuscule, scoffing and sorry for each other and ourselves.

One had to be passive in each follicle to understand.
Amidst the sound of rifles sighting in,
either night or owl snatching up what it did.

What we envisioned for ourselves was not this.
We were beauty our own.

SENTIMENTS OF SHOULD

To hold the Etruscan vase to your ear sounds
like the sea did millenniums ago, though incarceration
may immediately follow.
We are so many years beyond ourselves now,

placards where everything was.
Lo! On the candelabra of the body the head is right to burn.

Once I found a halo, which turned out to be the rim
of a truck I could barely lift.
So I sailed it into the fire station door and ran.

One can take so much and then only so much—

how the sun can smear everything to a sheen equivalent
to the coal-stoked eyes of deer on night's highway.

Or stated differently, if I were holding one
it would be impossible for me to put down the gun.

An ambulance is crashing. A boy with a manifesto
waits for school to start. Then the bandaged cities afterwards.

With heartache our opium, would we all be better off
as flowers? At what temperature
does the epithelium burst into glitter?

Absence begetting pressure begetting absence—

in the torrent of dying out, even a leaf hitting
the earth is devastating. Though it never had them,
the scarecrow wants its wings back.

IN RIPE WILDERNESS

There is blood so red it is black, horns
that double back to pierce their fecund animal source.
Outside, workers dig a pit

exposing the infrastructure, the hairline fracture and rusted main.
If you concentrate, can you feel yourself in
your sinuses, your spine?
Made of alabaster the body would be lighter.

In ripe wilderness (and I remember this clearly) where a man
slices his finger in the field, amidst
the hare's entrails & bloody mess, certain greens
emerge from other greens, truth
from THE TRUTH distinguishes itself.

Underfuckingestimated: the czarina in her brittle white coat,
loosestrife to propagate the tire tracks.

Liquids heavier than water pool on the ocean floor
so that, while submerged, further submergence is possible.
Years a person could go on with the head
sub or even unconscious.
At 20 below the nose hairs freeze into icy little slivers.

Dear intimates of the past and present, sorry for not loving you
more. Sad sunset, your melancholy here.

Equip us with feathers, hollow out the bones until they become
meager enough to float.
A man ventures into the world with a jacket and keys
and thinks that world his.

DUST OF A DESICCATED HORSE

When the bullet crashed from its celebratory shot
skyward, we found it in the morning
flattened on the concrete like a penny
squashed on the destitute tracks of the only route

out of here. Reading yourself to sleep hereafter
is impossible. Better to cloister yourself away
like a pigeon in the stockyard's corrugated eaves

where loneliness wrings its hue from the
parking lot's lights until there isn't even a shadow
to consult. Meaning the club-shaped hollow entity
wind tries to flog into song IS YOU.

Seeing the anonymous heart shelved in its mustardy
preservative, I thought it glimmered with the
singularity of a snowfield, a geography erased.
The quiet there—as though you could auscultate

the slow pulse of an oak
with your palm, hear the grasses moan when
a mushroom is plucked from the earth. How do we
account for the backdrop of factorylight

featuring the opportunistic overgrowth as enchanted
wood? And why shouldn't we
build a bonfire in the basement with flags for
surrender and plastic shrieks of optimism?

I wonder how it feels to be buried so long amidst
the pines, where the calves press
their casual heft earthward, returning a gesture.

It's sad. The present is rarely panoramic. When it is
you're too preoccupied with
the slaughterhouse of your past to notice.
To think you're horse dust, that

another broken nose is a only a function
of the clarity of the sliding glass doors. Which too,
are invisible to the birds

conferring in ellipses over the tenements, fluid
and dream-like, a testament
to the vaporous amniotic state between satisfaction
and longing, wherever it resides.

The forest, no doubt. Where you go, dragged
by the scruff of the neck, while
gypsy moths stitch the limbs of the trees together

and the dew-mist settles like smoke
from the demolition tinged air of the entire
freaking erstwhile century.

PLASTICITY

You would suspect birds and smokestacks are
opposed to one another, but they are not. Birds

form the equation of its circumference.
Inside, soot corrodes inwardly.
Outside, everything is meat chaos in the
thoroughfare, i.e., your chapped lips, charcoal colored

birds, the twilight prison yard yellow and
the smokestack overlording, if not anatomical.

When I passed the exploded car on the road's
shoulder, it was boot black outside, except
for the overture of crackling orange fusing mind to
matter, matter to mind to instant irreparable memory.

I kept driving, exhausted, in an excusably late neo-
Om kind of way. After that
you just want to lie down on the couch,

turn the laugh track on loud with your beleaguered
coordination and think of nothing.
Which it comes to show, is no less than
the out-there-everywhere.

I mean the time it takes just for water to boil,
for the woodlands to repopulate and
acquire again their smooth, frictionless sheen,

like I should be in constant pursuit of some ever-
returning to sincerity, that
I should mention here the baby
I have to take care of, except there is no baby.

That I should wake up early, resign myself to endless
amperes of radio politics and aphoristic primitivisms.

As meanwhile the dopey clouds caravan
(or convalesce) all Stevensian, anti-purposed and
prodromal-like through Hartford, that meta-city
same as anywhere—Kenosha, Tacoma,
Oswego. And so off we go, the astronomers

confident our realities are drifting ever apart,
and accelerating, that now is
never now enough, as I drip nachos on the page.

Making you think a sandwich is no small thing, that
a hangover is a cure for a hangover is homeopathic,

that I should get my birthmarks checked,
ride my bike to work,
that I should condition myself to be less conditional,
an astronaut, a soldier of fortune, a diplomat.

That much of the voice's tone is attributable to the
decorum and plasticity of the sinuses,
which is why the headvoice sounds
so otherly out loud.
Go ahead, hit me with an epiphany, it says

such that the woman entering her apartment drops
her Kevlar glove like an intentional future artifact
to define perfectly the aura of the era.

You would suspect the intensity of the sun would
burn holes through you, but it does not. Instead

you infect or you flower, I loosed to my students
freezing on the substrate of a Brooklyn sidewalk,
their eyes prodigiously empty as Baltimore.

THE CULTURE OF HANDGUNS

If postmodern culture be anything at all, it is surgery
to get in shape.

Second grade, the nuns hauled me to the office by my hair
because I didn't have a napkin with lunch.

Though I took a machete to school one Halloween
and it never made a scene.

It used to be that encountering frightened oxen on a suspension
bridge meant something. Distance
truncated now to only a required series of immunizations.

I've always believed karma to be a statistical science,
that even to call your life amorphous lends it a kind of shape,

though I've come to remember everything differently
than photographs suggest.

Does rain sharpen or dull as it falls? Where does one begin?—
to reinvent yourself, you must have somehow first
invented yourself.

Wars ensue between window displays. Smoking
is not allowed in the building, but the building itself smokes.

Who will be the first to give birth to a knife we muse,
to reduce anger to a sphere you can roll between your fingers,
sticky and black?

It has been long-established that the mind can hold itself
hostage, that we inherit each other.

Yesterday a man was held point-blank against a wall over there,
and we wonder now if he did it himself.

HAZE EXQUISITE

Not even modern death is that succinct.
As it goes, I leave the radio on to ghost the rooms when
I leave. In this vagrant neighborhood,

when I hear kids in discord-euphoria on the street
I want to tell them I too hate being splashed or

slapped in the head. It's misleading, the terroir between
putrefaction and exhaustion, between the reality of
chairs sitting there and the mystique of the senses.

You can't tell where the cinematic clouds let off
and the shit storm begins. Wrens polka dot the rims of
the factory stacks. Light infiltrates the cracks

prying everything open. Then evening in all its aplomb
and monochrome tides in translucent as onion-skin

obliterating any depth of field. One thing I know,
you can't rely upon the vestibular system. To tell yourself
one thing is for instinct to do another.

You can't ground yourself in someone declaring
they love you even if they do. Or did. Like after all the
lowland flooding and half the kennel was found hooked
to their chains in an overdraft of mud. From which

they pulled and pulled just to bury again. How do you
convince anyone that affixing jumper cables to their
nipples is not a story of ardor, that they shouldn't

go out and arsonize whatever they could? Just think
about the way it really is. The brutal themselves abused,

life sentences are proffered in sans serif fonts, deliberate
and devoid of any emotion whatsoever, and with the
slightest breeze you can discern open sky mouthing
a hunger. While go the fat rest of us

arm in arm, laughing and sanguine, entering and exiting
nothing but the sheer excellence of restaurants.

IT IS HARD TO BELIEVE IN THE SOUL

The little hairs in the lungs rust.
It is hard to imagine wind.
What is emptiness? A flower?
Whosoever's body is flush with the world is a god.

Where water pools in the shade your reflection trembles.
The woman on the balcony, you imagine her from yesterday.
Vines spill from banister to cement and you swear

the baby's eyelashes are silk, the river
tons of effluvia at once.
If anything, the soul is a series of invisible arches, mass
without weight, the smallest sense of moon-colored fortitude.

A ladder reaches the roof and keeps going.
The woman, she believes she is bread.
You too believe you are bread, that if anything
the flower is born inside out.

In the mind wild grasses pant and fold.
The broken colloquy of a hammer, thirst of trees
in your blood. The blue thread
you ease from your shirt to stitch air to air.

THE SKY AT GROUND LEVEL

The interminable meat machine is stuck on ON.
Someone keeps coughing, soiling the quiet in this room.
Can you hear the spear humming in its encasement?
It's honing in on its target.

And the skull, if history beaming back at us through its
hungry eyeholes were to tell us anything at all
it would say: Fetch me a piece of bread already, idiot!

For a long time in your life nothing matters,
then the wood bees return to nest in your porch,
and a glass of wine or two is all it takes
before you're confident you can saw someone completely in half
and piece them together on television.

Ditto the sun's rays bisecting the glass buildings,
which increasingly suggest construction nearer the clouds
is a symptom of turbulence on the asphalt below.

As if there were ancients among us. . . .
As if there was someone in the Antarctic of the mind
you needed to reach,
and fast. O hell it is to be remaindered from the psyche,
to get heckled and forget your lines mid-matinee!
(Hi Mom! Hi Dad!)

For the wrong person it can take a lifetime to
hang a picture in its right place. Practicing patience
is such that you can exhaust the rest of your existence
trying. Look at Poland now!

Isn't that what it's about—the mantis
indistinguishable from the tomato leaf,
forgiving your childhood floggers, orderliness at the airport?
These attributes will forever serve you.

Still, the sum of everyone's lifetimes together
equals nil. Not a number at all, but more of a place.
Here exactly, where square rain badgers
the ampersand temples, and even the deer, keepers
of dense eastern forest, oddly frequent the beach.

DESTINY STREET

Much more than being cold or wet, it is the loss
one feels in the event of rain, as though someone went out
and painted everything a darker shade
of its own lingering sentiment.

On the contrary, there are people like fire for example,
who exist solely for the rapture of their own consumption.

Known is that we are foreign in our bodies.
In terms of a hammer or nail or dead wood, which do you think
the heart? I have always thought
a lawn mustn't resemble a golf course necessarily.
But people do, just as

there are those who covet a sunburn once in a while.
Most of us would enjoy a shiny silver envelope in the mail
regardless of its contents,
would argue tattoos and pedicures are real sustenance.
Most contend the act of genuflecting is inherently genuine,

while standing on a chair imparts a kind of liberation,
not so much for the better view as its unlabeled usage.

Beneath the umbrella of a lit downtown,
the language of the moon on the brownstones' crawling vines
resides these days at a frequency to which only bats are attuned.

Astronomy, they say, is a dying culture anyway, reality
at best a tertiary experience.

That we are walking around
in the footsteps of at least a thousand people every day, that
we too are ghosts, already ancient,
while the room with the highest concentration
of art in most homes is the garage.

OTTO

Murder is one thing, misdemeanor another.
When the baby tornado touched down
it was exclusive to the horticulture of a single resident,

gifting tomatoes to the entire block.
There should be a drug to mimic such kindness,

or a leaf on which we could suck.
Did you ever suspect you were a grace note
in this ensemble, hail dinging off the billboard
where the bastardized ad reads *How to be a scandal*.

You feel kinship with someone you don't even know,
rescue too many cats to feed. Thus
the individual is devoured by the institution it serves.

Still, the high drama of watching the sunset remains,
whether for its calming tea-like attributes
or the verve incited by its incendiary plummet.
It goes either way, as if your name was Otto,

can't discern the highway northbound from south,
body from spirit. Though when you meet the real Otto

it's never who you'd imagined, just another dude
with a foreign accent and bad tattoos. To look
at a mountain then is to question its solidarity,
not to mention its solidity (if its core

is not hollowed out). Inside, someone plotting to
return us to the beginnings of civilization,
or graffiting the planet's most obscure locale.

More likely: a missile waiting for its attendee to dump
coffee on the button. Alongside of which is a metaphor

of the missile exploding the mountain into a confetti of
narcissi and geraniums, suggesting everything will be
alright, the valley now bathed in raw materials

for such an exquisite perfumery
that the local economy can flourish, and forget again
its history that there has never been
a name for what goes on here, just corpses.

CHANTERELLES

For them I set to the rain a stern pace.
How will we collect the mosquitoes? Were
her ovaries suspended in her torso like streetlights
the storm knocked out?

Last night's questions beamed with the celestial pitch
of a star in a cigar box.
Of chanterelles, their birth is slow and dark,
more mysterious than the body's,
a precipitation upward through the yellow hue of
some elemental industry.

The aphid sap-sucked the field. Butterflies
swarmed heaps of what the horse dropped.
We are lonely and desperate creatures wishing to be
loved now when we could remain intimates forever.

In how many waiting rooms did the magazine despot's
eyes peer softly, and tobacco brown?
There should be a place we could all swim naked in
the lake, forget what the hound's tooth forecasted.

When I saw the boy with gray hair sprinkling bread
in the pond, the park squirrels
seemed weighably less enthusiastic, the birches
in their sidewalk patches of peat, bleak and leafless.

We were landslides to each other.
There was no time for connoisseurship.
The dusky seaside sparrow was no longer, and so often
we pulled over to pupate from this vista or that.

Evening your favorite color, I kept imagining
the ceiling painted gold, while the beach we fetishized
was a pile of hot sawdust.
Strictly for the sun's burn did we reside.
You were the animal they warned you about.

PHASING OUT THE DEWCLAW

There are countless ways to embarrassment
or stardom. Hers was not closing the curtains

framing the exclamation of her figure like parentheses,
an aside to the confusion of evening, above which
the skyline begged for fireworks, operatic clouds.

Thankfully, you don't have to think about
putting on pants to go to the grocery store, though
sometimes you wish you knew a foreign language
so no one could understand.

Shouldn't our dialogue be as visceral as sideways rain?
The provisions for our well-being are boundless,
misses by the asteroids, a blade that can

pierce the car door and slice the tomato afterwards.
Do you feel lighter with each breath, stuffed further
with horsehair and springs?
Racing to extinction, it's the dewclaw vs. the appendix.

Artfully, insects attract to the sleeper's mouth.
Shakespeare and Cervantes alike thought death
was a form of sleep. Now we know
it's just the final payment on the body amortization.
Like what you get for pissing out the window,
a little blowback.

Between the left-for-dead and left-for-dead,
that's where you stand, realizing there never was
a rainbow in the rainbow room,

while the workers planting trees in
front of the condominium squint, triangulating
their position between the moon

tugging at their cells and the daily non-stop to Dubai,
the way the field at night sounds like an infant
breathing amidst the itch to erect an effigy.

BREATHING APPARATUS

There is the meat and there is the idea
of the meat. The tigress on TV
lingers over her kill just so.
Happiness is in the viscera, a swoon
in which the flies hover.

In the hotel lobby, cocktails are taken
for prissy little walks. It's more the posture
of the attire than the attire itself.
So many sparkly people render the air brighter
on your skin, makes the bloodshot Serengeti
an austere aphrodisiac.

There is air and there is the idea of air,
the tusk and the beard, the pheromones
and unaccounted-for moons.
What can still be imagined of the buildings'
reflection in the passing water,
the people in them flute music from
a vulture's wing bone?

The old woman through the crowd forgets
she already knows how to walk the stairs.
Alongside, the girl who could
hold her breath until she was robin's egg
blue, if a robin's egg were blue.

ADVERBIAL OF DIRECTION

In the dream the funeral pyre hovers like
a spaceship. Hail the skin its halogen aura, earthlight
and fatty shine.

As the fever puffed our little girl's face up, it was
clear we were hangers-on to the pink pearlized
ribbon on our way to the jet stream, our sporting
nerve running out.

The strike of the bullet before the sound of the shot
and the indefensible are pulverized. Simple as that.

And if the temple could levitate off its candlelit
postures of contrition, it would,
the way the fluorescent sticky note's sentiment of milk
and something scribbled out curls from the door.

You out there, the super-predator is man. It's true,
when you sneeze your soul exits and something lethal
comes in. Believe that.
A feeling like codeine, nothing anyone can do but

talk about the cucumber seedlings pushing up,
not what, but how silence floats, a facet of embryonic
law rendering us all subjects of subjects-of.

Should we go about recalculating our transgressions
or buying lottery tickets? Who could coax the trees

to generate a more amicable wind?
The weird totality of steam condensing in the window
of a Chinese Laundromat
scattered downwardly, reluctant rivers.

You come home to the same place a zillion times and
one day it's a foreign city,
the dead air broadcast of mist and gray
a viscous anthemic music for that in need
of rescue or allegiance.
As such, the mouths in our mouths know only want.

IN THE MERCURY OF ALL THINGS DISSOLVING

Two men carried an organ through the street, rain
making the sky corduroy. The orchid
adorned with just being there—it is not weight,
I thought, but awkwardness

that confounds us. Like the phone call
where you couldn't speak, letting silence instead
undo the imbroglio of your purple-black mood.
How then I was reminded of being firmly in Budapest

without having ever been: the architectures of austerity
and pure glaze of the sensation: where is there
such thing as time if there is now.

Thus I'm convinced our bodies have a memory like clay,
and I could be very good at the bassoon
because I've never tried. How often I think I'm just
a probability of ether, a trail of stray mathematics

scattered over the feral sidewalks of this city, finally
leading to your door. This Molotov of milk
and vinegar—*c'est moi?* Though conceived with

enough distance (and in retrospect), our existence seems
perfect, even if we are simply an idea of ourselves.
The tenements rising down into the puddles, the cut on
my finger throbbing, had the rain

all this while been a seething half-wind?
Still it was weird of the cars dreaming by for the road
to intone like meat. So often it seemed mist

was mistaken for mystique. Error presiding as
intention, it felt fortunate somehow,
truly fortunate that the next millennia would
fashion a necklace of our teeth.

THE NEW AUSTERITY

Spectacular is the ant's writhe under
magnifying glass, its slow collapse into itself.
Like ancient city, like spine.
O to be of the world a pin lofted by the water's tension!

Juxtaposed: the artful arrangement of meat
in the butcher's window,
the virgin boxing cream puffs in the *patisserie*.

How amazing it was that the crab grasses
never consumed us as we lay
gorged with idea, the moon pulsing up there, tenuous
as a hangover, shiny as a cure.
And the infant's coffin-cum-tool chest—if to exude was
to speak, its only two words were sad and sadder.

Routing through the cemetery revealed
that which was too heavy to topple was better suited
to spray paint,
while at the cash register, revulsion
often transpired into congenial glee.

Who isn't drawn to firelight? To the cartography of
a stranger's bright scar
to place them in the firmament of here and now?
And the foal with excess hair?
A condition thankfully none of us bear, privileged
as it appears.

The star-nosed mole saw with its scent.
Some species pursued the beautiful stink of another
to fatal exhaustion.
Best friends, we'd wager on
who'd get closer to the hornets, and understood death in
its gesticulations as the price of what remains
after everything is gone.

On the kind of day you could walk
the middle of the street, someone's broadcasting their
weeping need to be let in—

whatever it is, they're sorry.
The silled pigeons convene such that
there might be available a lot less love and money
than thought, and nothing sun or rain soaking to the
bone could make whole.

Teach me to step as a pine's shadow
across the forest floor.
Administer to me a boulder's patience for lichen.
The baby pushing out feet first proves
we are anomalies to one another.

GROSS ARDOR

After sophistications countryside, I craved shitty Mexican,
a soul from which to wring the accrued juice, aka experience.

I ambled around with a mass of coins in my pockets
to feel substantive. Rich and disturbing was the television
at night so that my gums bled.

I saw my life from the vista of twisting the nub
behind the dog's ear
until, unscrewed, it was a tick and fell into the rug's boiled nap,

sans anesthesia, needle-nose pliers extracting the meat of my thumb,
missing the splinter entirely.
How long could surviving make due on toast and cigarettes?
The olive tree was bent in the very question.

To want the mead is to chew the honeycomb with the bees
Heisenberg would have said,
that at the level of the phenomena, humidity
was inseparable from heat, heat from delirium to the same degree

that one thrived in the altitude at which they were born.
All I wanted was to set something
aflame, if only for its hypnotic grandeur:

order eating chaos eating order.
Until the authorities showed up. Until it became too much
the gross ardor of missing someone,

like mint quietly overrunning the garden.
I never locked eyes with the hillside's wild boar.
I had come into the world not knowing and would leave as such.

Flowers like burst capillaries everywhere,
I knew it would require the absolute behemoth of a man
to be the scalded child's palliative.
Indeed there was so much aftermath to be done.

THE MASTERY OF MOVING ON

The body amphora, the body free rent, the body
if only briefly. Good people, unzip your spines and lie
limp with me. Listen,

there are so many things we can never reveal until
one of us is on a death bed, until the various
unthinkables happen and part we must.
As Christ's ribs were pierced, I wonder if all his intentions

went leaking out into atmosphere. How the leaves look
plumped up with indecipherable, yet all-important
gesture, meanwhile, everyone summery and belief-suspended.
Meanwhile, *The Guns of Navarone*. As it happens,
something innocuous as cloud cover will change your

mind entirely, like the storm after which the houses and trees
aren't where they're supposed to be, victims
and volunteers alike, indistinguishable.
Already I miss you and the bones in my throat feel

out of place. It's inevitable we rarefy ourselves into
something we can no longer live with.
By now we should be pedaling our sorry asses home

or tucking into a hardy lunch, humbled and downcast.
When the drunk guy sat next to me and bought me
a drink, I was obliged to thinking a simpler world was in order.
As in, who could turn the asparagus stench of summer's
garbage piling up into happy?

And, where have all the alchemists gone?
We need them. To understand so much of what is known
turns out to be a symptom of vertigo. Lust

festers into disgust, into a job-like almost petrochemical funk.
Above it all, the sun making you sneeze, askance
as an asterisk up there, implying you in everything

so that everywhere a body of water came
near (her only solace) she had to dip her feet in it.

OVER CONVERSATION

Not everything dreams.
By the time the arsenal is built, it is expired.

Someone is always seeking an ethos to bleed.
Nausea occurs even via placebo.
In this life, you must have the tenacity of a tick
with mammoth tusks.

Still, a leaf grazing the pavement mimics
a door creaking open. Eventually, the mystery
of being alone consumes itself.
There are no other eras.

Filed away as memory, memory dissipates
into atmosphere. Then why shouldn't speech
from one latitude to another,
between us,
appropriate the muscularity of clouds?

What throbs in the bushes is not a bird,
but bird-like, neither gravity nor mystique.
Something pulls us so,

and closer to admiration for the tirelessness
of weeds, for the falling world.

ACKNOWLEDGMENTS

Grateful acknowledgment is made to the following publications in which these poems first appeared or are forthcoming:

At Large:
Beneath the Face is a Ball Peen Hammer
Destiny Street
In the Hemisphere Between Quest and Conquest

Caffeine Destiny:
It Is Hard to Believe in the Soul

Hunger Mountain:
Chanterelles
The Loveliest Cities

Hotel Amerika:
From Gulls Salvaging Open Air to Hyperventilation

Clade Song:
Dust of a Desiccated Horse
Migrations Wrested
Over Conversation

Forklift, Ohio:
In Ripe Wilderness
Haze Exquisite

B O D Y:
Phasing Out the Dewclaw

Bill Rasmovicz is the author of *The World in Place of Itself* (Alice James Books, 2007) and *Idiopaths* (Brooklyn Arts Press, 2013). His poems have appeared in *Hotel Amerika*, *Nimrod*, *Mid-American Review*, *Third Coast*, *Gulf Coast* and other publications. A pharmacist, he has also served as a workshop co-leader and literary excursion leader throughout much of Europe. His current home is Brooklyn.